NISTIR 7504
June 2008

Usability Testing of Height and Angles of Ten-Print Fingerprint Capture

Mary Theofanos
Brian Stanton
Charles Sheppard
Ross Micheals
Nien-Fan Zhang
John Wydler
Larry Nadel
William Rubin

Table of Contents

1. INTRODUCTION 7
2. METHOD 8
    2.1 PARTICIPANTS 9
    2.2 MATERIALS 10
        2.2.1 Digital Fingerprint Scanners 10
        2.2.2 Adjustable Platforms 11
        2.2.3 Adjustable Table 11
        2.2.4 Capture Software 12
    2.3 PROCEDURE 12
3. RESULTS 13
    3.1 USABILITY METRICS 13
    3.2 EFFICIENCY 14
    3.3 EFFECTIVENESS 19
        3.3.1 Individual Finger NFIQ 20
        3.3.2 Frequency of Individual Finger NFIQ Scores 22
        3.3.3 Summary 24
    3.4 OVERALL QUALITY 24
        3.4.1 Thumb Quality 25
    3.5 USER SATISFACTION 26
4. DISCUSSION 33
5. CONCLUSIONS AND FUTURE WORK 34
6. REFERENCES 35
APPENDIX A: POST TEST QUESTIONNAIRE 36
APPENDIX B: MEDIAN NFIQ SCORES FOR HEIGHT FOR ALL ANGLES 39

List of Figures

FIGURE 1 FREQUENCY OF COUNTER HEIGHTS IN TRIAL AIRPORTS 8
FIGURE 2 AGE RANGE OF PARTICIPANTS 9
FIGURE 3 HEIGHT (WITH SHOES) OF PARTICIPANTS 10
FIGURE 4 ANGLED SCANNER WITH PEGS 11
FIGURE 5 ADJUSTABLE TABLE 12
FIGURE 6 TIMING FOR SCANNER A 15
FIGURE 7 TIMING FOR SCANNER B 16
FIGURE 8 MEDIAN TOTAL TIMES FOR SCANNER A 18
FIGURE 9 MEDIAN TOTAL TIMES FOR SCANNER B 19
FIGURE 10 FINGER NUMBERING 20
FIGURE 11 INDIVIDUAL FINGER MEDIAN NFIQ FOR ANGLES (REPRESENTATIVE OF ALL PARTICIPANT DATA) 21
FIGURE 12 REPRESENTATIVE DISTRIBUTIONS FOR ANGLES (FINGER 3) 23
FIGURE 13 US-VIST QUALITY SCORING 25
FIGURE 14 US-VISIT QUALITY SCORES 25
FIGURE 15 MOST COMFORTABLE ANGLE 27
FIGURE 16 LEAST COMFORTABLE ANGLE 27
FIGURE 17 TALL PARTICIPANT STRUGGLING AT 39 IN. AND 30° 28
FIGURE 18 SHORTER PARTICIPANT STRUGGLING AT 49 IN. AND 0° 29
FIGURE 19 HANDS PRESSED TOGETHER 30
FIGURE 20 THE THENAR REGION OF THE HAND 30
FIGURE 21 GRASPING THE SCANNER 31
FIGURE 22 FINGERPRINT ROTATION MEASUREMENT 31
FIGURE 23 FREQUENCY OF THUMBPRINT ROTATION 32
FIGURE 24 ROTATED THUMB PRINT EXAMPLE 32

EXECUTIVE SUMMARY

The Department of Homeland Security (DHS) and the United States Visitor and Immigrant Status Indicator Technology (US-VISIT) program is preparing to transition from a two print capture process to a 10-print slap capture process. In preparing for the 10-print pilot testing, a concern that the existing counters that house the fingerprint scanners are too tall to support the ten print collection process was identified. Lowering the counters in the facilities is not possible for the pilot testing. However, angling the scanners on the counter may alleviate the problems. US-VISIT asked the National Institute of Standards and Technology (NIST) Biometrics Usability team to examine the impact on fingerprint capture performance of angling the fingerprint scanners on the existing counter heights to accommodate the upcoming pilot testing.

The NIST Biometrics Usability group's study[1] was specifically designed to answer the question: Given the current counter heights in US-VISIT facilities, what is the "best" angle to position the fingerprint scanner? The study included three metrics:

1. Efficiency – the time to complete the tasks. Does the angle of the fingerprint scanner affect the time required to capture fingerprint images?
2. Effectiveness – how good are the prints? Does the angle affect the quality of the captured images?
3. Satisfaction – comfort. Do users prefer a particular fingerprint scanner angle?

The installed base of counter heights at the US-VISIT facilities ranged from 83.9 cm (33 in.) to 124.5 cm (49 in.). Previous research on work surface heights and fingerprint capture recommended a counter height of 91.4 cm (36 in.). This experiment was designed to test the taller counter heights, specifically the most common counter height of 39 in., the tallest counter height of 49 in. and the midpoint of 114.3 cm (45 in.). Two fingerprint scanners were also provided by US-VISIT, each had a height of 15.2 cm (6.0 in.).

The experimental procedure is summarized as follows. One-hundred and twenty-six NIST employees participated in the experiment. Each participant was instructed to complete five tasks: left slap followed by left thumb, right lap followed by right thumb, and both thumbs simultaneously. Fingerprint images were collected from each participant at the four different angles for one counter height (i.e. the experimental design for angle was within subject and

---

[1] These tests were supported by the Department of Homeland Security. Specific hardware and software products identified in this report were used in order to perform the evaluations described. In no case does such identification imply recommendation or endorsement by the National Institute of Standards and Technology, nor does it imply that the products and equipment identified are necessarily the best available for the purpose

for height was between subject). The order of the angles was counterbalanced and the right and left start conditions were randomly selected.

The study population ranged in age from 17 to 67 mirroring the US-VISIT population. The population was also representative with respect to U.S. population height based on data from the Centers for Disease Control and Prevention (CDC).

This report describes five main results.

1. there is no significant effect on efficiency (time) due to angle or counter height (only the left slap for one scanner was found to be significant with respect to counter height);
2. there is no significant effect on effectiveness (quality) due to angle for either scanner, but significant differences were found across different counter heights, the effect of which appears to be scanner dependent;
3. there is no significant effect for subject height except for right slap, left slap, and both thumbs for scanner B.
4. the effect on user satisfaction is a function of the counter height, angle, and subject height;
5. participants overwhelmingly prefer to start the capture process with their right hand; and
6. participants tend to extend their four fingers around the scanner when positioning both thumbs resulting in rotated thumb print images.

Accommodating visitors of different heights with an adjustable counter height is not possible for the 10-print pilots. This study suggests that angling the scanner will improve user satisfaction (i.e., customer service); however, no overall improvement in transaction time or image quality should be expected.

1. INTRODUCTION

The Department of Homeland Security (DHS) and the United States Visitor and Immigrant Status Indicator Technology (US-VISIT) program are migrating from a two print capture process (left and right index fingers) to a 10-print slap capture process (all fingers on both hands). This transition is based in part on recommendations from the National Institute of Standards and Technology (NIST) that were made in the joint report to Congress titled "Summary of NIST Patriot Act Recommendations" [6]. There is a concern that the existing counters that house the fingerprint scanners are too tall to support the 10 print collection process. Lowering all of the counters in all of the facilities is not possible at this time. But US-VISIT hypothesized that angling the scanners on the counter may alleviate the problems. US-VISIT asked the NIST Biometrics Usability team to examine the effects on fingerprint capture performance of angling the fingerprint scanners on the existing counter heights.

The NIST Biometrics Usability group performed an experiment to evaluate positioning fingerprint scanners at different angles.[2] The study was specifically designed to answer the question: Given the current counter heights at US-VISIT, what is the "best" angle to position the fingerprint scanner? In this case best included three measures [4]:

4. Efficiency – the time to complete the tasks. Does the angle of the fingerprint scanner affect the time required to capture fingerprint images?
5. Effectiveness – how good are the prints? Does the angle affect the quality of the captured images?
6. Satisfaction – comfort. Do users prefer a particular fingerprint scanner angle?

A review of the literature on standards for design and anthropometric measurements such as MI STD 1472 [5] provided little guidance on proper angles for fingers or palm placement. These standards focus on line of sight and reach envelopes including sloping control panels for cockpits or nuclear power stations. We were unable to locate any applications that included angling devices for palm or finger placement. However, there is guidance on angling computer keyboards [2][5][9][10]. This research focused on angling the keyboard between -15 and +15 degrees. Simoneau and Marklin [9] found that changes in wrist angle are influenced by sloping the keyboard or by adjusting the height of the support surface thus modifying the wrist position relative to the elbow. Thus the relationship of the wrist to the

---

[2] These tests were supported by the Department of Homeland Security. Specific hardware and software products identified in this report were used in order to perform the evaluations described. In no case does such identification imply recommendation or endorsement by the National Institute of Standards and Technology, nor does it imply that the products and equipment identified are necessarily the best available for the purpose

keyboard varies according to the height and angle. This finding was particularly relevant to our study, since previous research on fingerprint applications had determined that the surface height of the fingerprint scanner can impact fingerprint performance [12]. Fingerprint performance degraded as surface height increased.

2. METHOD

US-VISIT provided the range and frequency of usage of the counter heights at the pilot facilities. The counter heights ranged from 83.8 cm (33 in.) to 124.5 cm (49 in.) (Figure 1 Frequency of Counter Heights in Trial Airports). The most frequently occurring height was 99.1 cm (39 in.) US-VISIT also provided the two fingerprint scanners to test. Both scanners were 15.2 cm (6 in.) tall. Previous research on work surface heights [13] and fingerprint capture recommended a counter height of 91.4cm (36 in.) for a six inch scanner. Taking into account the previous recommendations, this experiment was designed to test the taller counter heights, specifically the most common counter height of 99.1 cm (39 in.), the tallest height of 124.5 cm (49 in.), and the "practical" midpoint of 114.3 cm (45 in.) (there were no counter heights at 111.7 cm (44 in.) at the facilities).

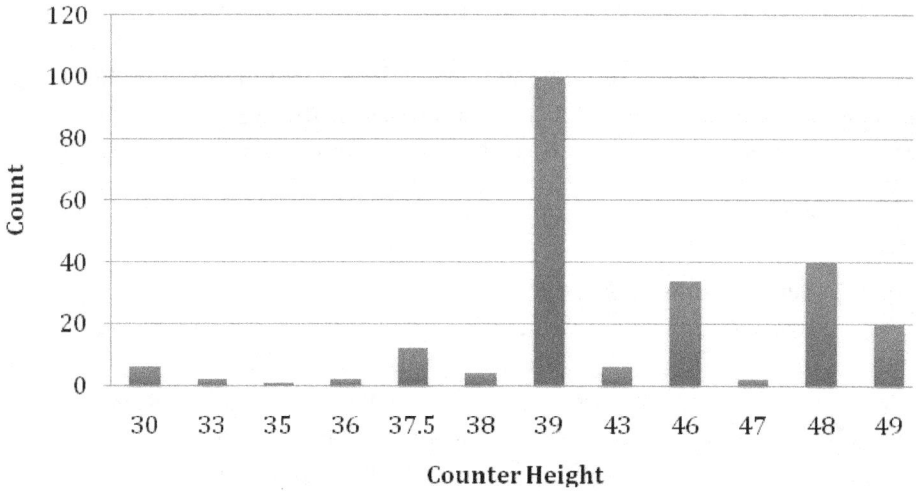

Figure 1 Frequency of Counter Heights in Trial Airports

The experiment was designed to accommodate 95 % of the population represented by the range from the 95th % male (186.7 cm or 6' 2".) to the 5th % female (152.8 cm or 5' 2") [5]. We used computer aided design (CAD) software to determine the test conditions for plausible angles. Using the CAD software, we modeled a scanner at the three counter heights through a range of angles against the target population. Applying these ranges in the CAD models revealed that an angle greater than 30° would be extremely difficult for participants six feet and taller. The models suggested four angles to evaluate: 0°, 10°, 20° and 30°.

2.1 PARTICIPANTS

The participants were 126 NIST employees who volunteered to participate in the study. There were a relatively equal number of men and women who participated and the ages were fairly uniformly distributed.

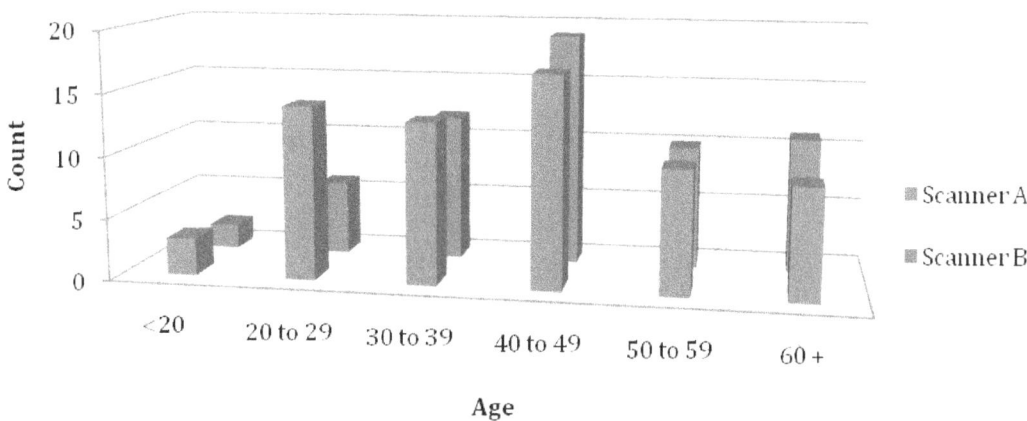

Figure 2 Age Range of Participants

The participants ranged in height with shoes from 149.86 cm (4' 11") to 198.12 cm (6' 6"). The mean height for scanner A was 165 cm (5' 5") for women and 175 cm (5' 10") for men, for scanner B: 167.64 cm (5' 6") and 175.26 cm (5' 9") for women and men respectively. The heights were fairly normally distributed. According to the Centers for Disease Control and Prevention (CDC) [1] the mean individual height of men is 175 cm (5' 10") and the mean individual height of women is 160 cm (5' 3") in the US without shoes, verifying that our population was representative. According to the World Health Organization the worldwide mean individual male height is 173 cm (5' 8") and the female height is 158 cm (5' 2") without shoes.

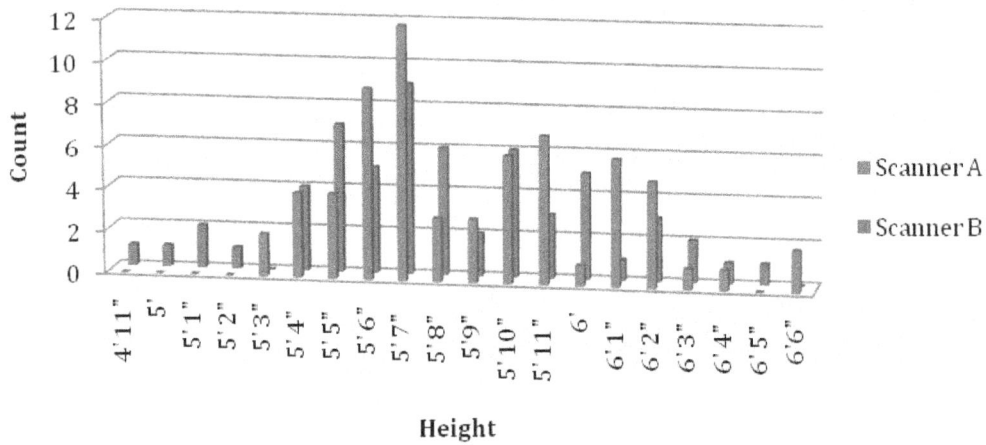

Figure 3 Height (with shoes) of Participants

Most of the participants were right-handed. For scanner A 88% were right-handed and 12% left or ambidextrous, for scanner B, 80% were right-handed and 20% were left or ambidextrous. The distribution is very representative of the general population [8] where 87% of the general population is right-handed.

2.2 MATERIALS

The experiment consisted of:
- two digital four-print (slap) fingerprint scanners
- adjustable platforms for the scanners allowing the scanners to be positioned at various angles
- adjustable tables that allowed for accurate positioning of the height
- custom software.

2.2.1 Digital Fingerprint Scanners

Two different fingerprint scanners were provided by US-VISIT. Each measured approximately 152mm (6.0 in.) by 152mm (6.0 in.) by 152mm (6.0 in.) .Thus the effective height of the scanner platen was 152mm (6.0 in.) above the work surface height. One of the scanners had a six degree slope built into the platen. US-VISIT indicated that they would not negatively angle the scanner to adjust for that slope in the field. Therefore, we did not compensate for that scanner at zero degrees but did account for the six degrees in the remaining angle calculations and positioning. Both scanners had Light Emitting Diode (LED) indicators on the top surface of the scanner. The LED indicators were not used in the study, since each scanner used them differently. They were covered on one of the scanners and were not obvious on the other. Each emitted audible tones during the scanning process that were not part of the study design.

2.2.2 Adjustable Platforms

An adjustable platform for the scanners was designed and built out of Plexiglas. This platform allowed the scanner to be positioned at various angles using pegs, as illustrated in (Figure 4 Angled Scanner with Pegs). The pegs were built to adjust the platform such that the scanner platen angle measured 10°, 20°, or 30°. Using Velcro, the scanner was attached to the platform. The angle was measured with respect to the platen and the counter top using a protractor.

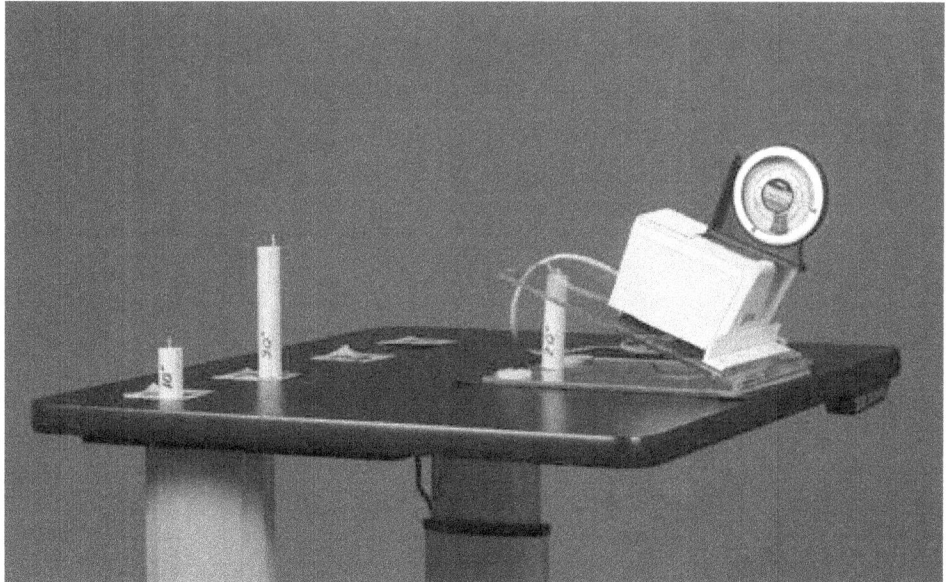

Figure 4 Angled Scanner with Pegs

2.2.3 Adjustable Table

Adjustable tables allowed for accurate positioning of the height as illustrated in Figure 5 Adjustable Table. The three heights of 99.1 cm (39 in.), 114.3 cm (45 in.) and 124.5 cm (49 in.) were pre-programmed into the table's height buttons. The height was measured from the floor to the base of the scanner accounting for the adjustable platform.

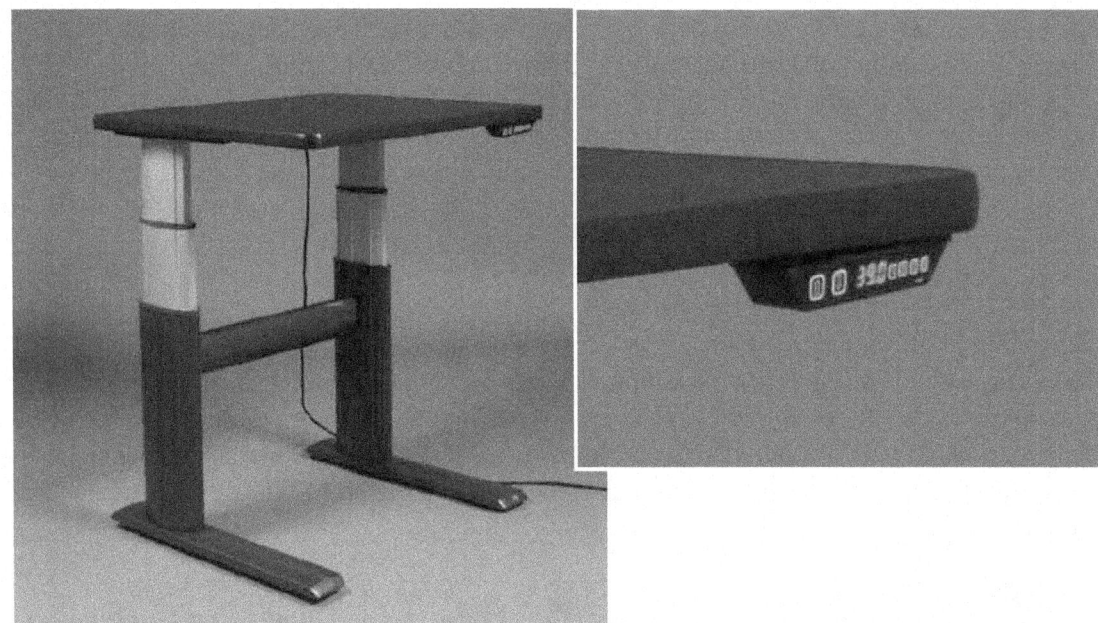

Figure 5 Adjustable Table

2.2.4 Capture Software

A custom capture application provided for controlled capture of images from a given user at the various heights and angles. The custom software's high-level operational flow is described in the following six steps:

1. Operator is prompted to adjust the scanner to a particular angle
2. Participant is prompted by an audio prompt for a slap/finger combination
3. Once the slap/finger is detected, images are captured
4. Repeat steps 2 and 3 for next slap/finger combination until all remaining combinations are captured
5. Repeat step 1 to 4 for any remaining experimental angles

The software application used the auto-capture algorithm and image capture calls provided by the vendors.

2.3 PROCEDURE

Each participant was instructed to complete five tasks. First, participants were asked to present a left slap followed by a left thumb or a right slap followed by a right thumb (known as a 4-1-4-1 slap). Once, both hands and single thumbs were collected they were prompted for both thumbs simultaneously. Fingerprint images were collected from each participant at the four different angles for one counter height (i.e. the experimental design for angle was within subject and for height was between subject). The order of the angles was counterbalanced (all possible combinations of angles were accounted for) and the right and left start conditions were randomly selected.

The order of presentation of the slaps was provided to the participants as verbal instructions generated by the software. Participants could not see the computer monitor. Before scanning was initiated, the operator adjusted the scanner to a given height and the flat angle and cleaned the platen. Participants' demographic data was collected and their height was measured. Next, participants received verbal instructions and a demonstration of how to position fingers on the platen for proper fingerprint capture from the test facilitator.

Before the test began each participant performed a "practice run" to become comfortable with the process, the voice prompts of the software, and the feel of the platen. Participants were instructed by the software to place a hand on the scanner and hold until the software prompted them to remove their hand. We did not explicitly indicate which hand to place on the scanner for this trial run, so that the user's natural preference could be observed. When the trial run was completed, the operator was prompted by the software to adjust the angle.

Once the adjustments were completed, the operator signaled the start of the trial. The participant listened to the system generated instructions and then placed the appropriate fingers on the platen for collection of fingerprint images. When an image was detected and captured the participant was instructed to remove his/her hand/finger from the scanner platen. This process was repeated for each task until all of the tasks for a given angle had been collected. Once all tasks for that angle were collected, the operator manually re-adjusted the scanner angle as prompted by the software for subsequent trials. When all tasks were completed at all four angles, the participant completed the satisfaction questionnaire (Appendix A).

3. RESULTS

3.1 USABILITY METRICS

According to ISO 9241-11 [4], usability is defined as "the extent to which a product can be used by specified users to achieve specified goals with effectiveness, efficiency and satisfaction in a specified context of use". The standard identifies three areas of measurement: effectiveness, efficiency, and user satisfaction, where

- efficiency is a measure of the resources expended in relation to the accuracy and completeness with which users achieve goals. Efficiency is related to productivity and is generally measured as task time
- effectiveness is a measure of the accuracy and completeness with which users achieve specified goals. Common metrics include completion rate and number of errors.
- user satisfaction is the degree to which the product meets the users' expectations—a subjective response in terms of ease of use, satisfaction, and usefulness.

In this study, we used the ISO definition and measured efficiency, effectiveness, and user satisfaction.

3.2 EFFICIENCY

We measured efficiency as the time required to complete a task, where a task is defined as a right-slap, left-slap, both thumbs, or each single thumb. Each task was initiated by a voice prompt and a timestamp was recorded when the software prompted the user to "please place your hand on the scanner". The software native to the scanner detected the image and determined if the image was acceptable. When the scanner signaled that it had an image our software ended the capture, recorded an end-capture timestamp and prompted the user to remove his/her hand as illustrated in Figure 6 Timing for Scanner A. For Scanner B the timing was slightly different. We found that we were unable to save the image while the hand was on the scanner. Thus for Scanner B the system ends the attempt and then the image is saved and a timestamp recorded, Figure 7 Timing for Scanner B. All times were recorded in milliseconds.

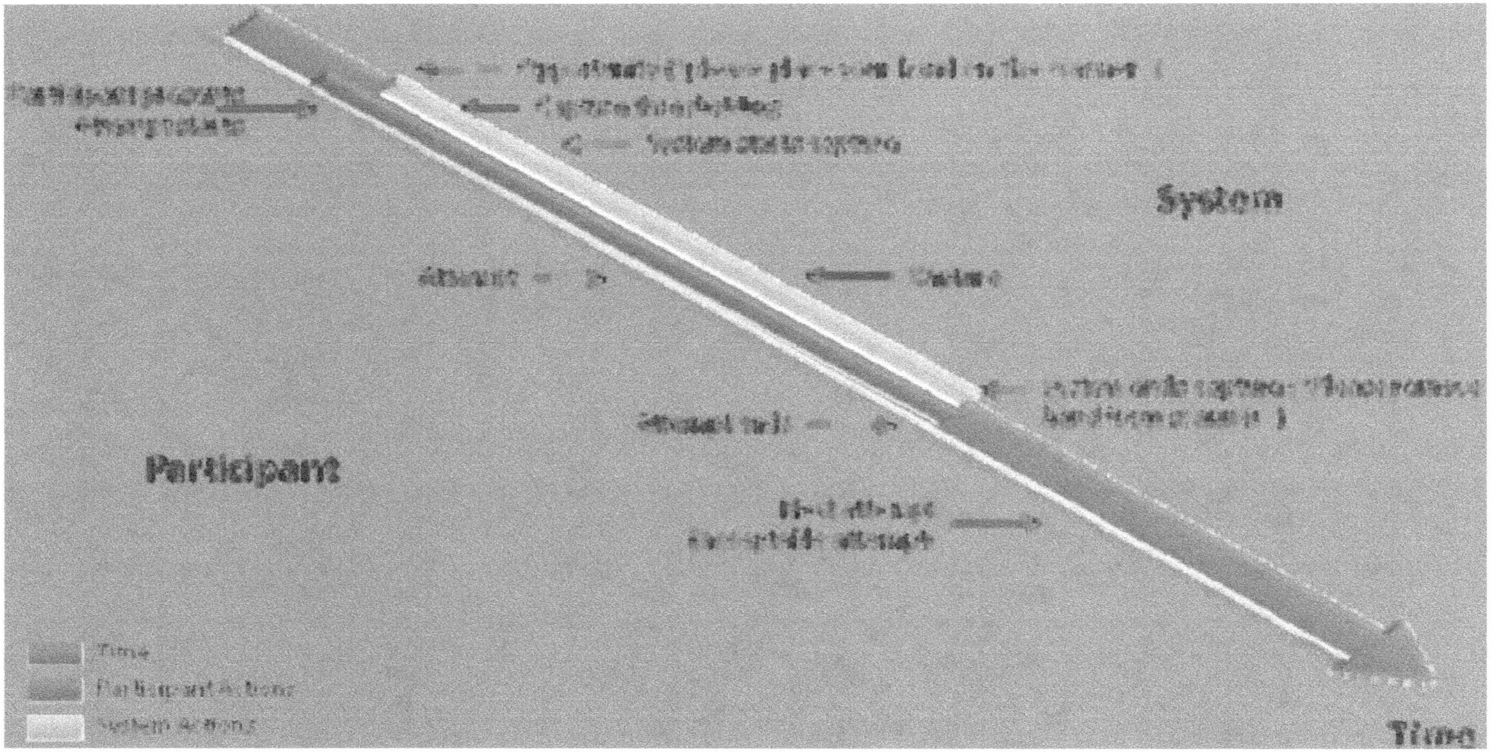

Figure 6 Timing for Scanner A

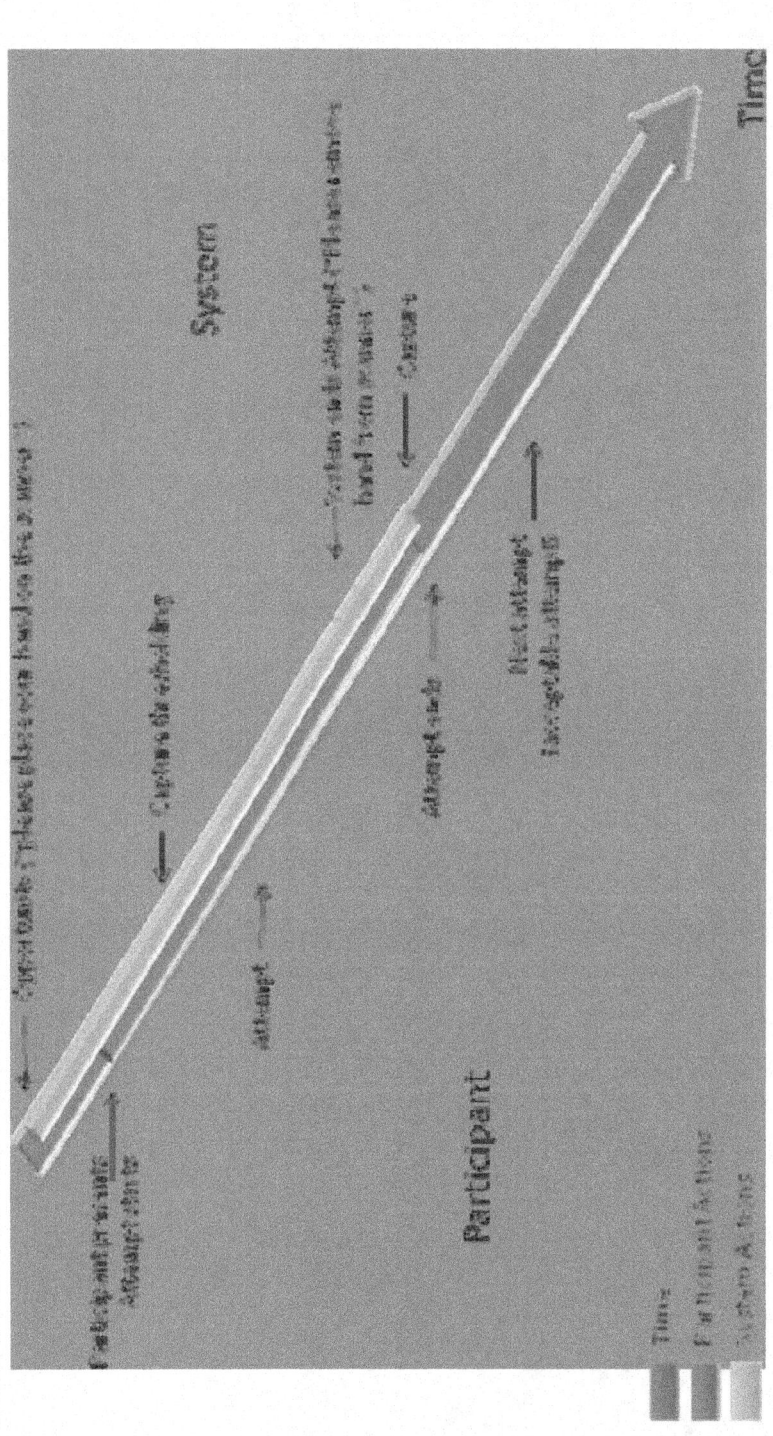

Figure 7 Timing for Scanner B

A variety of independent variables composed the experiment. There were five tasks Task 1:right slap, Task 2: right thumb, Task 3: left slap, Task 4: left thumb, and Task 5: both thumbs. For each task there is a response variable of time. There were three table heights: 99.1 cm (39 in.), 114.3 cm (45 in.), 124.5 cm (49 in.). Four angles were used for each table height: Flat, 10°, 20°, and 30°. Two scanners were used for the experiment. For Scanner A, a total of 66 people were tested, 22 for each table height. Similarly for Scanner B, a total of 60 people were tested, 20 for each table height. Demographic data such as age, participant height, handedness, and start hand are also considered in the analysis.

For each response variable of time for each task we examined the factors of angle, counter height and participant height. The timing data was not normally distributed therefore we used medians and non-parametric tests such as Kruskal-Wallis. For Scanner A we found no statistically significant differences for the factors of angle, table height, and subject height as illustrated in Table 1 Scanner A: Significance for Time ("+" : $p<0.05$). Significance is indicated by "+" for $p < 0.05$ and not significant by "-".

Task	Angle	Table Height	Participant Height	Median Time
1 right slap	-	-	-	10.03
2 right thumb	-	-	-	10.53
3 left slap	-	-	-	10.00
4 left thumb	-	-	-	10.01
5 both thumbs	-	-	-	10.03

Table 1 Scanner A: Significance for Time ("+" : $p<0.05$)

Task	Angle	Table Height	Participant Height	Median Time
1 right slap	-	-	+	16.83
2 right thumb	-	-	-	16.81
3 left slap	-	-	+	16.87
4 left thumb	-	+	-	16.85
5 both thumbs	-	-	+	11.38

Table 2 Scanner B: Significance for Time ("+" : $p<0.05$)

For Scanner B the factors of angle and table height were also found to have no statistically significant differences in the test results except for Task 4: left thumb. The Kruskal-Wallis test indicates that the effect of table height is significant with p=0.01. In addition, the subject height was significant for Task 1:right slap, Task 3:left slap, and Task 5:both thumbs.

To summarize the data indicates there is no significant effect due to angle for time required to complete a fingerprint task for either scanner. There was no significant effect due to table height with respect to the time required to complete a fingerprint task except for the collection of left thumb for scanner B. Finally, there was no significant effect for subject height except for right slap, left slap, and both thumbs for scanner B.

For illustrative purposes, we include the median total times of two slap sequences for each scanner. We calculated the time for a 4-1-4-1 slap sequence and for a 4-4-2 sequence (where hands are presented one at a time followed by simultaneous thumbs). It is important to note that these total times do not include the time between tasks but only the cumulative time to capture each individual slap. The times range from 40.66 s to 46.37 s (4-1-4-1) and 31.41 s to 45.97 s (4-4-2) for scanner A as illustrated in
Figure 8 Median Total Times for Scanner A. For scanner B the times range from 67.46 s to 61.74 s (4-1-4-1) and 38.28 s to 45.51 s (4-4-2) (Figure 9 Median Total Times for Scanner B). As expected the 4-1-4-1(four slaps) sequence requires more time than the 4-4-2 (three slaps) sequence. In [13] we report on the total time a participant required to complete the slap sequences, from receiving the instructions to capturing the final slap; the mean times ranged from 146 s to 163 s and the median from 127 s to 152 s for the 4-4-2 slap sequence.

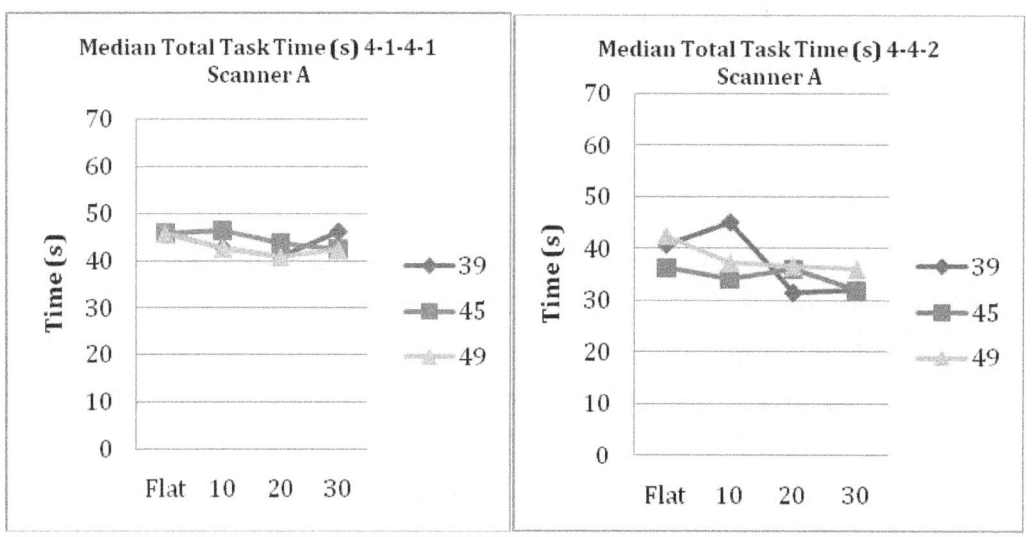

Figure 8 Median Total Times for Scanner A

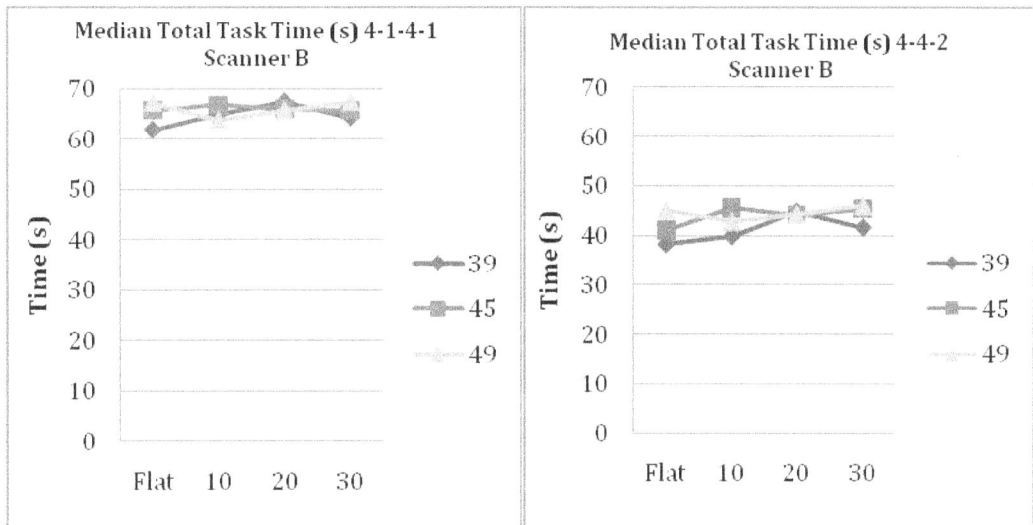

Figure 9 Median Total Times for Scanner B

3.3 EFFECTIVENESS

Effectiveness examines the quality of the capture images. How good are the captured image? Which variables (angle, counter height, subject height) impact the quality of the images. The analysis of effectiveness or the quality of the captured images is based on image quality as formally defined by the NIST Fingerprint Image Quality metric, or NFIQ [11]. We captured slap images and used the NIST fingerprint imaging software to segment the slaps into individual fingers and compute the NFIQ score for each finger. NFIQ scores range from 1 to 5. NFIQ is rank based and lower values correspond to higher quality. We collected 12 prints per angle for all four angles at three heights for two scanners and 126 people for a total of 5,760 prints.

The analysis used the Federal Bureau of Investigation (FBI) numbering for fingers for the right and left slaps, and the individual thumbs task. For the simultaneous thumbs task the right thumb was assigned to 11 and the left thumb was assigned to 12 as indicated in Figure 10 Finger Numbering.

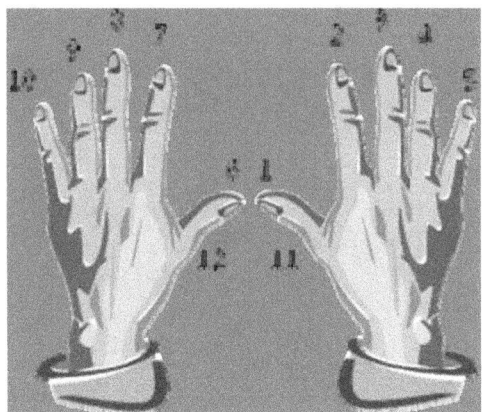

Figure 10 Finger Numbering

For completeness since there is not yet consensus in the biometrics community on how to determine the quality of a slap image, to study the impact of angle, counter height, and subject height we performed the analysis two ways. The first approach compares the NFIQ scores of individual fingers. Using this approach a median NFIQ score is calculated for each finger across each task. But since NFIQ scores are discrete values from 1 to 5 it may not be appropriate to calculate the medians, the frequency of NFIQ values for individual fingers was determined. This approach examines the distribution of these frequencies across a task to determine quality differences.

3.3.1 Individual Finger NFIQ

The second approach compares the NFIQ scores of individual fingers. Using this approach a median NFIQ score is calculated for each finger across each task. Performing the analysis with respect to each individual finger we found no statistically significant differences for angle for Scanner A or Scanner B. Figure 11 Individual Finger Median NFIQ for Angles illustrates that the median NFIQ across all tasks and heights for each angle were not significant for either scanner.

Figure 11 Individual Finger Median NFIQ for Angles (Representative of all Participant data)

For Scanner A table height was found to be significant using the Kruskal-Wallis test for all fingers except 6 (left thumb), 11 (right thumb from both thumb task), and 12 (left thumb from both thumb task) shown in (T1 = 99.1 cm (39"), T2 = 114.3 cm (45"), T3 = 124.5 cm(49)") Table 3 Quality Effects of Table Height - Scanner A. The median scores for each finger are presented in Appendix B.

Finger #	Task #	Table height	Angle
2	1	+. T1>T2. T2<T3	-
3	1	+. T1>T2. T2=T3	-
4	1	+. T1>T2. T2=T3	-
5	1	+. T1>T2. T2=T3	-
7	3	+. T1>T2. T2=T3	-
8	3	+. T1>T3. T2=T3.	-
9	3	+. T1>T2. T2=T3.	-
10	3	+. T1>T2. T2=T3.	-
1	2	+. T1>T2. T2<T3.	-
6	4	-	-
11	5	-	-
12	5	-	-

(T1 = 99.1 cm (39"), T2 = 114.3 cm(45"), T3 = 124.5 cm(49)")
Table 3 Quality Effects of Table Height - Scanner A

For Scanner B table height was found to be significant for fingers 1(right thumb), 4 (right ring finger), and 10 (left little finger) using Krusdal-Wallis as indicated in (T1 = 99.1 cm (39"), T2 = 114.3 cm(45"), T3 = 124.5 cm(49)")* marginally accepted with p=0.0508.
Table 4 Quality Effects of Table Height - Scanner B . The median scores for each finger and the threes heights are provided in Appendix B.

Finger #	Task #	Table height	Angle
2	1	-	-
3	1	-*. T1>T2. T2=T3	-
4	1	+. T1<T2. T2<T3	-
5	1	-	-
7	3	-	-
8	3	-	-
9	3	-	-
10	3	+. T1<T2. T2<T3.	-
1	2	+. T1>T2. T2<T3.	-
6	4	-	-
11	5	-	-
12	5	-	-

(T1 = 99.1 cm (39"), T2 = 114.3 cm(45"), T3 = 124.5 cm(49)")* marginally accepted with p=0.0508.
Table 4 Quality Effects of Table Height - Scanner B

3.3.2 Frequency of Individual Finger NFIQ Scores

Finally we examined the distributions of the NFIQ for angle and the table heights with respect to each finger. Using this approach the number of occurrences of each NFIQ value for each finger is determined. Once these frequencies were computed for each finger across the angles and table heights a chi-square test was used to investigate the significance of the differences among the distributions of quality scores. We found that for all fingers the no significant differences were found. In other words, the distribution is the same across the angles for both scanners. Figure 12 shows the distributions for finger 3.

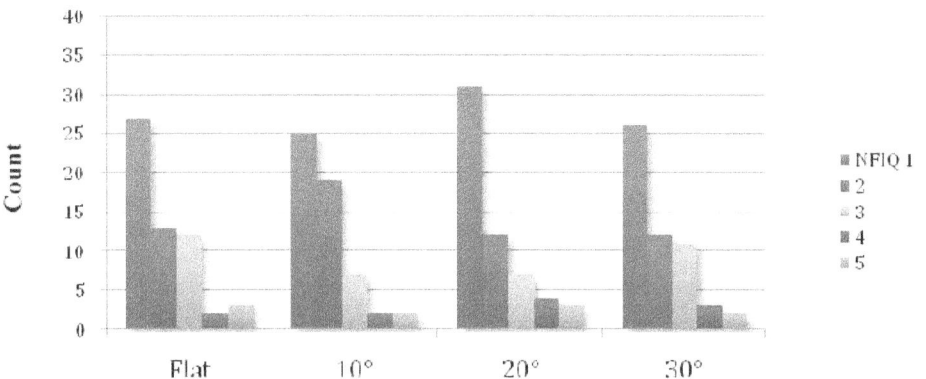

Figure 12 Representative Distributions for Angles (Finger 3)

But once again we conclude that counter height is significant for some fingers for both scanners. For Scanner A, except for fingers 5,6,11,12, the distribution of NFIQ for each finger is different for different table heights as illustrated in Table 5 Scanner A Table Height NFIQ Distributions * indicates significance.

Finger #	Chi-square value	p-value
2	31.36	0.0001*
3	32.34	0.0001*
4	21.91	0.0051*
5	14.03	0.08
7	27.01	0.0007*
8	33.70	0*
9	30.56	0.0002*
10	28.61	0.0004*
1	20.48	0.0087*
6	12.23	0.1411
11	13.69	0.09
12	14.54	0.0688

Table 5 Scanner A Table Height NFIQ Distributions * indicates significance

For Scanner B, we conclude that except for fingers 1,6,11,12, the distribution of NFIQ for each finger is different for different table height as shown in Table 6 Scanner B Table Height NFIQ Distributions * indicates significance.

Finger #	Chi-square value	p-value
2	19.51	0.01*
3	27.15	0.0007*
4	33.57	0*
5	22.23	0.0045*
7	17.81	0.02*
8	22.88	0.0035*
9	30.98	0.0001*
10	27.01	0.0007*
1	4.23	0.38
6	12.16	0.14
11	9.30	0.32
12	12.59	0.13

Table 6 Scanner B Table Height NFIQ Distributions * indicates significance

3.3.3 Summary

In summary, there is no significant difference in quality due to angle for either scanner irrespective of which method used to analyze the data. Significant differences were found among table height. However, the results were mixed between scanners. The affect of table height appears to be scanner dependent and requires further study.

3.4 OVERALL QUALITY

In order to characterize the overall quality of the images we used a proposed quality scoring method under consideration by US-VISIT. Using this method a slap is accepted (meaning it is not necessary to attempt to capture another image) if the index finger, middle finger, and thumb has an NFIQ value of 1 or 2, and the ring finger and little finger have an NFIQ score of 1,2 or 3 as illustrated in Figure 13 US-VIST Quality Scoring. The results of applying this criteria are shown in Figure 14 US-VISIT Quality Scores. We collected approximately 480 images for each slap. Of the 480 images for the right slap only 58 % for Scanner A and 63 % for Scanner B met the acceptance criteria. The left slap had the lowest percentages, 55 % for Scanner A and 60 % for Scanner B.

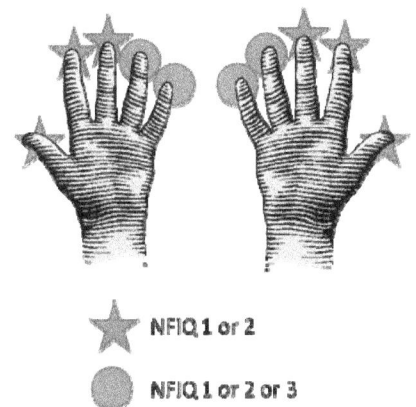

Figure 13 US-VIST Quality Scoring

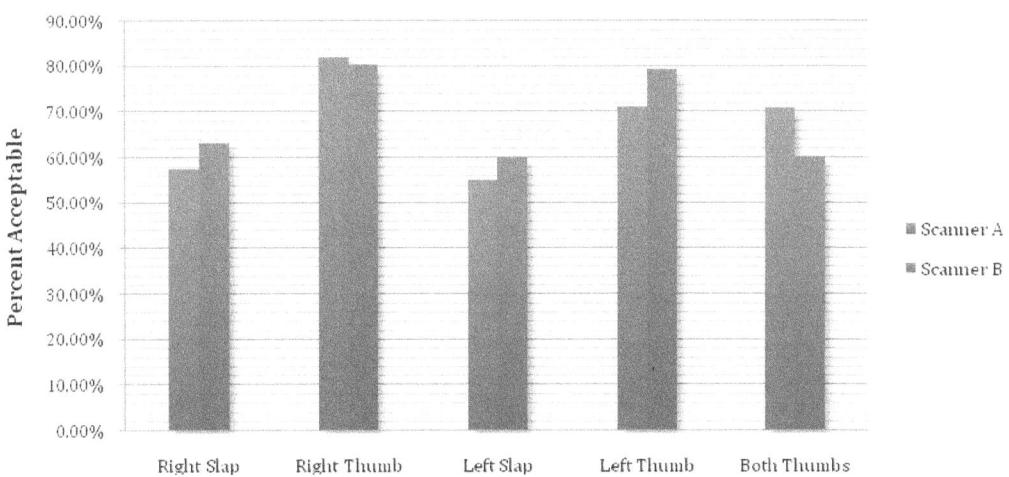

Figure 14 US-VISIT Quality Scores

3.4.1 Thumb Quality

In a previous study on counter heights [12] we observed a decrease or drop in quality from individual thumbprints to simultaneous thumbs. The data indicated that individual thumbs give higher quality images across all heights. An examination of the quality of individual thumb prints versus simultaneous thumbs collected in this study confirms our previous finding. As reflected in Table 7 NFIQ Scores between Solo Thumbs and Simultaneous Thumbs - Scanner A, the individual thumb prints were of higher quality for each counter height except for right thumb at the 45 in. counter height. The results for Scanner B are presented in Table 8 NFIQ Scores between Solo Thumbs and Simultaneous Thumbs - Scanner B. For Scanner B we found no significant difference in quality for the right thumb at any of the counter heights, but the left single thumb was found to have higher quality than the quality of the simultaneous left thumb at two of the counter heights.

	99.1 cm (39")	114.3 cm (45")	124.5 cm (49")
Finger 1 vs. finger 11	$q_1 > q_{11}$ $P<0.05$	$q_1 = q_{11}$ $P=0.51$	$q_1 > q_{11}$ $P<0.05$
Finger 6 vs. finger 12	$q_6 > q_{12}$ $P<0.01$	$q_6 > q_{12}$ $P<0.05$	$q_6 > q_{12}$ $P<0.01$

Table 7 NFIQ Scores between Solo Thumbs and Simultaneous Thumbs - Scanner A

	99.1 cm (39")	114.3 cm (45")	124.5 cm (49")
Finger 1 vs. finger 11	$q_1 = q_{11}$ $P=0.45$	$q_1 = q_{11}$ $P=0.06$	$q_1 = q_{11}$ $P=0.66$
Finger 6 vs. finger 12	$q_6 > q_{12}$ $P<0.01$	$q_6 > q_{12}$ $P<0.01$	$q_6 = q_{12}$ $P=0.45$

Table 8 NFIQ Scores between Solo Thumbs and Simultaneous Thumbs - Scanner B

3.5 USER SATISFACTION

Each user was given a satisfaction survey after completing the test. The questions included:

1. Which angle did you find most comfortable?
2. Which angle did you find least comfortable?
3. Please rank the angles in order of preference: 1 is most preferred, 4 is least preferred.
4. When prompted for your thumbs, which method did you prefer?
5. Did you have difficulty positioning yourself for any of the trials?
6. Any additional comments on how we can improve the fingerprint capture process?

The complete questionnaire is found in Appendix A.

In general for both scanners as the counter height increased, more people preferred a steeper angle as shown in Figure 15 Most Comfortable Angle. Figure 16 Least Comfortable Angle provides the data for least comfortable angles.

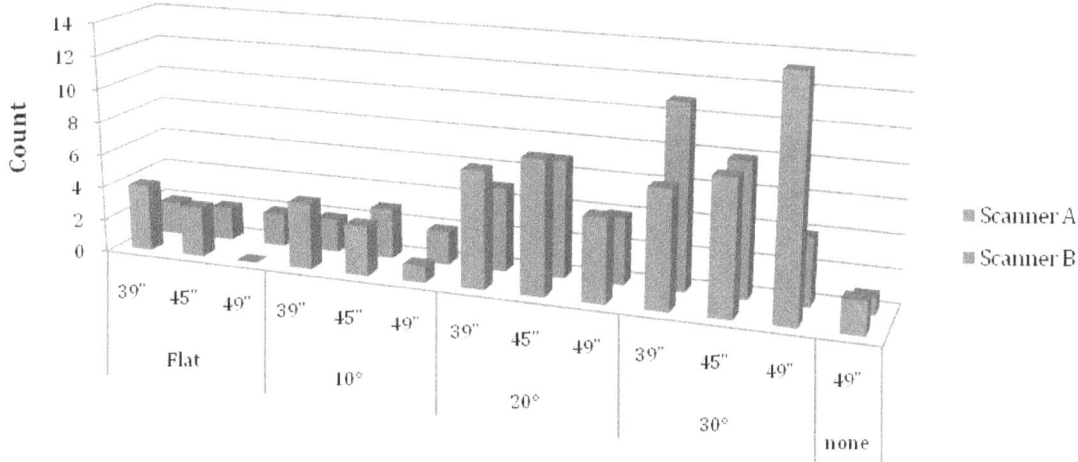

Figure 15 Most Comfortable Angle

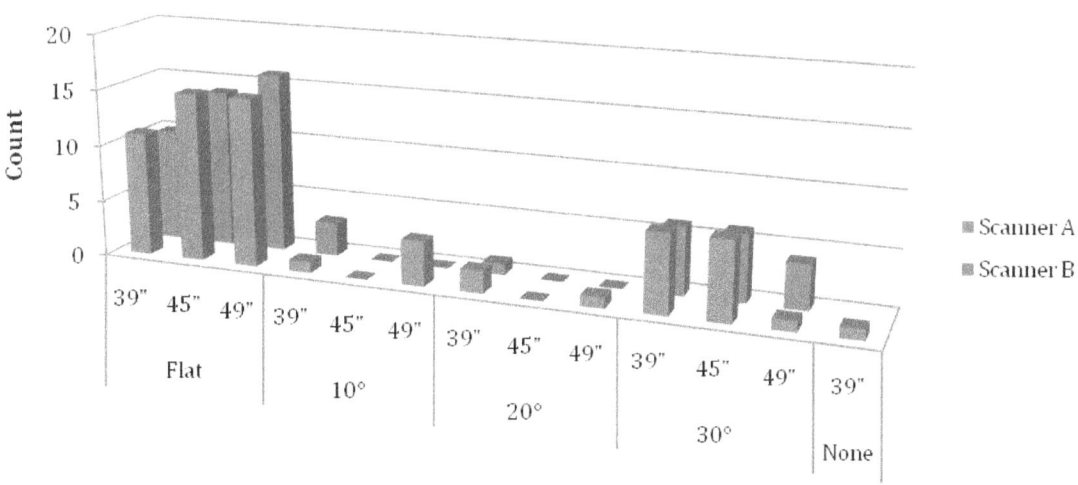

Figure 16 Least Comfortable Angle

The least comfortable angle appears more dependent on the participant's height. Shorter participants indicated that the flat angle was the least comfortable while taller participants indicated that the 30° angle was least comfortable. Figure 17 Tall Participant Struggling at

99.1 cm (39 in.) and 30° illustrates the difficulty a taller individual experienced at the 99.1 cm (39 in.) counter height and an angle of 30° while Figure 18 Shorter Participant Struggling at 124.5 cm (49 in.) and 0° shows a participant that was 158 cm (5' 2") struggling to position both thumbs at the 49 in. counter height and Flat. Only a few participants identified the 10° or 20° angles as uncomfortable.

Figure 17 Tall Participant Struggling at 99.1 cm (39 in.) and 30°

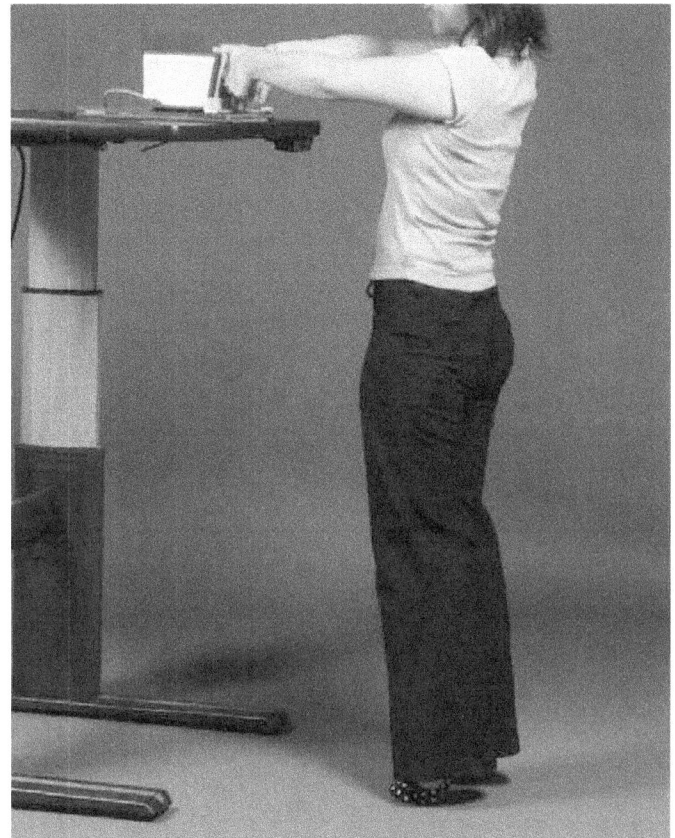
Figure 18 Shorter Participant Struggling at 124.5 cm (49 in.) and 0°

Finally, as the height of the counter increased, more people preferred single thumb prints to positioning both thumbs together (Figure 19 Hands Pressed Together). This preference was further elaborated in the participants comments. In response to "Did you have difficulty positioning yourself for any of the trials?", most of the comments were about positioning the thumbs. They also indicated that it was uncomfortable to place both thumbs simultaneously. Comments included "this is awkward" and "kind of hard."

Even though each participant only experienced one counter height and we asked no direct questions concerning the counter height many participants commented on the counter height. Of the 40 people who participated at the 124.5 cm (49 in.) counter height 50 % commented that the table was too high and should be lowered. We observed that most participants shifted their weight or stepped from side to side to position themselves before placing their hand on the scanner. We also observed that many people especially for Scanner B extended their 4 fingers on each side of the scanner in order to position their two thumbs simultaneously on the platen at 30°. Finally, many participants scrunched or lifted their shoulders and fully extended their arms or elbows in order to press down with both thumbs.

Participants positioned themselves using one of two methods to capture their two thumbs simultaneously. These methods appear to be scanner dependent. For Scanner A most participants held their fists together with their thumbs extended as illustrated in Figure 19 Hands Pressed Together.

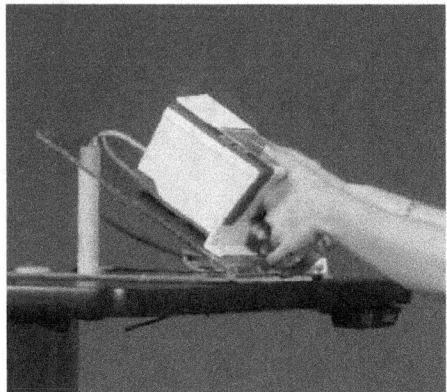

Figure 19 Hands Pressed Together

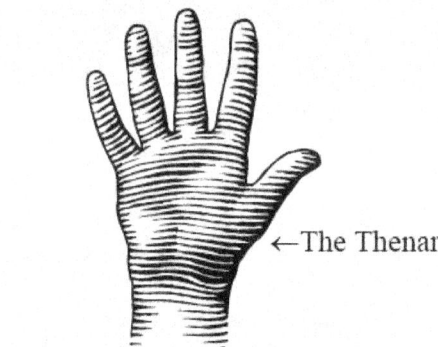

Figure 20 The Thenar Region of the Hand

In general, pressing the wrists or the thenar region of the hands, together provided balance and stability as the images were collected. For Scanner B most participants were unable to press their thenars together. As a result we observed many participants extending their four fingers on each side of the scanner (Figure 21 Grasping the Scanner) for stability and comfort during the scan.

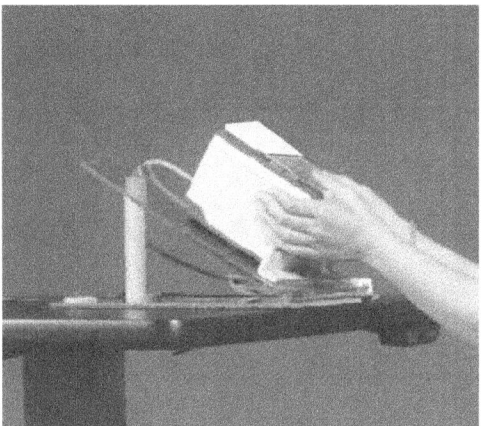

Figure 21 Grasping the Scanner

We observed that this behavior resulted in the rotation of the thumbs from perpendicular and this rotation may prevent capturing the fingerprint core. We examined and measured the rotation of the thumbs. We used the FBI standard to measure thumb rotation and used the crease of the thumb to determine perpendicular and an overlay as illustrated in Figure 22 Fingerprint Rotation Measurement.

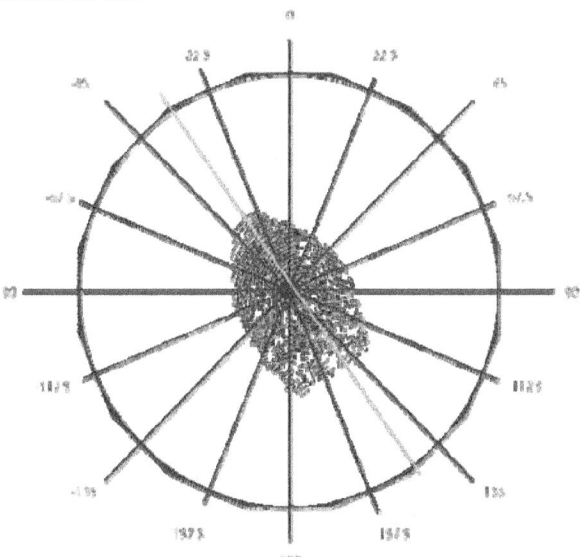

Figure 22 Fingerprint Rotation Measurement

The thumb rotation for scanner A was consistent across all heights and angles as shown in Figure 23 Frequency of Thumbprint Rotation.

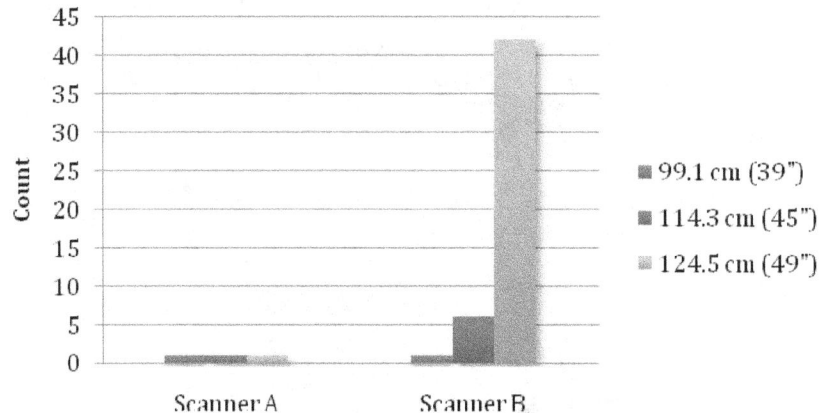

Figure 23 Frequency of Thumbprint Rotation

Thumb rotation for scanner B was not consistent across all counter heights and angles (Figure 23 Frequency of Thumbprint Rotation). As the height increased the number of participants who rotated their thumbs increased and the amount of rotation increased. In fact one person positioned his thumbs completely backwards or 180°. Even though participants were rotating their thumbs, there were very few images without the cores. Of the 480 two thumb prints only two were missing the cores for Scanner A and four for Scanner B.

*Prints have been altered for privacy protection

Figure 24 Rotated Thumb Print Example

Finally participants prefer to start the scanning process with their right hand as observed from the "practice run". As described above, before the test began each participant performed a "practice run" to become comfortable with the process. Participants were instructed by the software to place a hand on the scanner and hold until the software prompted them to remove their hand. We did not explicitly indicate which hand to place on the scanner for this trial run For the practice or trial run we found that overwhelmingly participants placed their right hand on the scanner. For scanner A, 79% of the participants preferred their right hand while 82% preferred their right hand for Scanner B.

4. DISCUSSION

This study examined the impact of angling fingerprint scanners at taller counter heights to assist users in positioning for the proposed 10-print fingerprint collection process of US-VISIT. We compared counter heights of 99.1 cm (39 in.), 114.3 cm (45 in.), and 124.5 cm (49 in.) and angled the scanners at Flat, 10°, 20°, and 30°. We used two scanners which were 152 mm (6.0 in.) tall resulting in a scanner platen height that was 152 mm (6.0 in.) above the counter. In a controlled environment, we collected images of a right slap, left slap, right thumb, left thumb, and both thumbs simultaneously. We did not attempt to simulate a Port of Entry or the stress associated with traveling and encountering the fingerprint process.

We found that angling the fingerprint scanners had no impact on quantitative performance. There was no significant difference in time to complete the tasks -- the angles had no effect. Nor did the angles affect the quality of the captured images irrespective of which method we used to identify fingerprint quality.

However, the counter height does affect the quality of the images confirming our previous research [11]. The counter height was not found to be a significant factor in time to complete the tasks. We observed mixed results between the scanners and between the approaches used to analyze image quality. The influence of counter height on image quality appears to be scanner dependent.

Participant height was not found to be a significant factor in time to complete the tasks. We observed mixed results between the scanners and between approaches used to analyze the image quality with respect to participant height. But,
participants clearly preferred the 20° and 30° angles as the counter heights increased. We observed that shorter participants struggled less at the taller counter heights when the scanners were angled. Very few participants indicated that they preferred the scanners to be flat on the counter surface. When given a choice participants overwhelmingly preferred to start the capture process with their right hand.

Finally, we observed that many participants extended their four fingers on each side of the scanner in order to position their thumbs for the scan. This approach to positioning thumbs increased as the height of the counter increased especially for Scanner B. This positioning results in captured images where the thumbs are rotated.

5. CONCLUSIONS AND FUTURE WORK

This study is part of a larger effort to develop usability guidelines for interacting with biometric hardware and software. Although the US-VISIT program has a great deal of operational data on the two print capture process, little data is available on a ten (slap) fingerprint image capture process.

This study was specifically designed to focus on the impact of angles on the process. We found that:
- there is no significant effect on efficiency (time) due to angle or counter height (only the left slap for one scanner was found to be significant with respect to counter height);
- there is no significant effect on effectiveness (quality) due to angle for either scanner, but significant differences were found across different counter heights, the effect of which appears to be scanner dependent; and
- the effect on user satisfaction is a function of the counter height, angle, and subject height.

We also found that participants overwhelming prefer to start the capture process with their right hand. Finally, participants tend to extend their four fingers around the scanner when positioning their thumbs resulting in rotated thumb print images.

In conclusion, we found that angle is not a factor but counter height is. However, this study cannot identify the "best" counter height for the US-VISIT scanners and environment. Additional research is required to address that question. Additional research is also required to determine the number of participants who will position their hands around the scanner and rotate their thumbs and the impact of thumb rotation on image quality. A pilot test in an operational environment would provide additional valuable data to establish guidelines.

Since retrofitting the existing counters with adjustable height mechanisms to accommodate visitors of different heights is not possible at this time; for the taller counters, if US-VISIT wishes, it can angle the scanner simply to improve user satisfaction (i.e., customer service); however, no overall improvement in transaction time or image quality should be expected.

6. REFERENCES

[1] "Advanced Data From Vital and Health Statistics", US Department of Health and Human Services Centers for Disease Control and Prevention, October 27, 2004, http://www.cdc.gov/nchs/data/ad/ad347.pdf

[2] Gilad, I., Harel, S. Muscular effort in four keyboard designs. *International Journal of Industrial Ergonomics* 26, 1 (2000), 1-7.

[3] Hedge, A., Powers J. R. Wrist postures while keyboarding- Effects of a negative slope keyboard system and full-motion forearm supports. *Ergonomics S* 38, 3 (1995), 508-517.

[4] International Organization for Standards. *ISO 9241-11 Ergonomic requirements for office work with visual display terminals (VDTs) - Part 11: guidance on usability* Geneva, Switzerland: Author, (1998).

[5] MIL-STD-1472F, Human Engineering Design Criteria for Military Systems, Equipment and Facilities. Department of Defense, 23 August 1999.

[6] National Institute of Standards and Technology. *Summary of NIST Patriot Act Recommendations.* Gaithersburg, MD. Retrieved January 4, 2007 from http://www.itl.nist.gov/iad/894.03/pact/NIST_PACT_REC.pdf

[7] Nelson, JE; Treaster, DE; Marras, WS. Finger motion, wrist motion and tendon travel as a function of keyboard angles. *Clinical Biomechanics 15,* 7 (2000), 489-498.

[8] Porac, C., Coren, S. *Lateral Preferences and Human Behavior.* Springer-Verlag, NY, 1981.

[9] Simoneau, GG; Marklin, RW. Effect of computer keyboard slope and height on wrist extension angle. *Human Factors* 43, 2 (2001), 287-298.

[10] Suther, T.W., McTyre, J. Effect on Operator Performance at Thin Profile Keyboard Slopes of 5 degree , 10 degree , 15 degree , and 25 degree. Proc. of the Human Factors Society 1982, Human Factors Society Press, (1982), 430-434.

[11] Tabassi, E., Wilson, C., and Watson, C. *Fingerprint Image Quality, (NISTIR 7151),* August 2004, http://www.itl.nist.gov/iad/894.03/fing/fing.html.

[12] Theofanos, M., Orandi, S., Micheals, R., Stanton, B., & Zhang, N. *Effects of Scanner Height on Fingerprint Capture (NIST IR 7382),* 2006, http://zing.ncsl.nist.gov/biousa/

[13] Theofanos, M., Stanton, B., Orandi, S., Micheals, R., & Zhang, N. *Usability Testing of Ten-Print Fingerprint Capture (NIST IR 7403),* 2006, http://zing.ncsl.nist.gov/biousa/

[14] Tilley, A. *The Measure of Man and Woman.* John Wiley & Sons, Inc., NY, USA, 2002.

APPENDIX A: POST TEST QUESTIONNAIRE

Demographic Questionnaire

1. Age
☐ Years

2. Gender
☐ Male
☐ Female

3. Handedness
☐ Right Handed
☐ Left Handed
☐ Ambidextrous

☞ **Please tell the test coordinator that you are ready to have your height recorded.**

For Subject #: _____

Date and Time of Trial: _____
Height of Table: _____

---

4. Height

☐ Feet   ☐ Inches

---

5. Which did you find most comfortable?

☐ 1st angle
☐ 2nd angle
☐ 3rd angle
☐ 4th angle

---

6. Which did you find least comfortable?

☐ 1st angle
☐ 2nd angle
☐ 3rd angle
☐ 4th angle

---

7. Please rank the following in order of preference by writing a 1, 2, 3 or 4 next to each. 1 is most preferred, 4 is least preferred.

☐ 1st angle
☐ 2nd angle
☐ 3rd angle
☐ 4th angle

8. When prompted for your thumbs, which method did you prefer?

☐ Both thumbs at the same time
☐ One thumb at a time
☐ No preference

9. Did you have difficulty positioning yourself for any of the angles?

☐ No
☐ Yes, please elaborate on the difficulty you had:

10. Any additional comments on how we can improve the fingerprint capture process?

APPENDIX B: MEDIAN NFIQ SCORES FOR HEIGHT FOR ALL ANGLES

Finger #	Table height	Median of NFIQ
1	1	2
	2	1
	3	2
2	1	2
	2	1
	3	2
3	1	3
	2	1
	3	1
4	1	2
	2	1
	3	2
5	1	3
	2	2
	3	2
6*	1	2
	2	2
	3	2
7	1	2
	2	1
	3	1
8	1	3
	2	1
	3	1
9	1	2
	2	1
	3	1
10	1	3
	2	2
	3	2
11*	1	1
	2	1
	3	1
12*	1	1
	2	1
	3	1

* Statistically significant by Kruskal-Wallis test

Table 9 Median Individual Finger NFIQ Scores by Table Height (Scanner A)

Finger #	Table height	Median of NFIQ
1	1	2
	2	1
	3	2
2*	1	2
	2	2
	3	2
3**	1	2
	2	1
	3	2
4	1	1
	2	1
	3	2
5*	1	2
	2	2
	3	2
6*	1	2
	2	2
	3	2
7*	1	2
	2	1
	3	2
8*	1	1
	2	2
	3	2
9*	1	2
	2	2
	3	2
10	1	2
	2	2.5
	3	3
11*	1	2
	2	2
	3	2
12*	1	1
	2	1
	3	1

* Statistically significant by Kruskal-Wallis test
** Marginally statistically significant by Kruskal-Wallis test

Table 10 Median Individual Finger NFIQ Scores by Table Height (Scanner B)

www.ingramcontent.com/pod-product-compliance
Lightning Source LLC
Chambersburg PA
CBHW081804170526
45167CB00008B/3321